Anorexia

Perspectives on Mental Health

by Bonnie Graves

Consultant:
Claire Mysko, Administrative Director
American Anorexia Bulimia Association

LifeMatters
an imprint of Capstone Press
Mankato, Minnesota

LifeMatters Books are published by Capstone Press
PO Box 669 • 151 Good Counsel Drive • Mankato, Minnesota 56002
http://www.capstone-press.com

Printed in the United States of America

Library of Congress Cataloging-in-Publication Data
Graves, Bonnie B.
      Anorexia / by Bonnie Graves.
            p.   cm. — (Perspectives on mental health)
      Includes bibliographical references and index.
      Summary: Describes the causes and characteristics of anorexia nervosa, an eating disorder, and offers strategies for dealing with your own and others' anorexia.
      ISBN 0-7368-0431-5 (book) ISBN 0-7368-0440-4 (series)
      1. Anorexia nervosa—Juvenile literature. [1. Anorexia nervosa. 2. Eating disorders.] I. Title. II. Series.
      RC552.A5 G72 2000
      616.85'262—dc21   99-056214
                                                CIP

Staff Credits
Marta Fahrenz, Judy L. Stewart, editors; Adam Lazar, designer; Jodi Theisen, photo researcher

Photo Credits
Cover: ©Capstone Press/Adam Lazar
Index Stock Photography/17, 21, 26, 58
International Stock/©Bill Stanton, 6
Photri, Inc./©David Lissy, 39; ©Skjold, 43
Photri/Microstock/15
Unicorn Stock Photos/©Jeff Greenberg, 23, 31; ©Martin R. Jones, 46
Uniphoto Picture Agency/©Michael A. Keller, 9, 40; ©Ed Elberfeld, 48; ©Llewellyn, 55; ©Bob Daemmrich, 56
Visuals Unlimited/©Jeff Greenberg, 11

A 0 9 8 7 6 5 4 3 2 1

Table of Contents

Anorexia nervosa is a serious eating disorder. People with anorexia starve themselves because they think they are fat.

People with anorexia can have health problems. Anorexia can damage organs and bones and cause heart problems.

Bulimia and binge-eating disorder are two other types of eating disorders. People with bulimia eat and then purge. People with binge-eating disorder overeat but do not purge.

The teen years are a time of growth and change. These changes can put teens at risk for anorexia.

Anorexia is a serious health condition, but it can be cured.

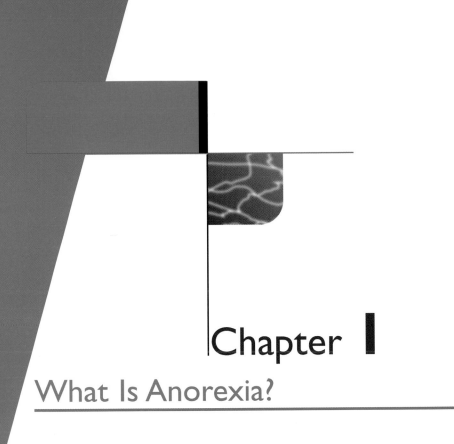

Chapter 1

What Is Anorexia?

Jennifer stood in front of the mirror. "You're fat," she told

JENNIFER, AGE 15

herself. Then she noticed that she could count every one of her ribs in the mirror. That made her feel better. Jennifer was 5 feet 6 inches tall and weighed 95 pounds. Every morning she got up at 5:00 to run five miles. She weighed the food she ate. She counted every calorie. Her goal was to lose a few more pounds. Maybe then she wouldn't feel fat.

Anorexia Nervosa

Jennifer has an eating disorder called anorexia nervosa, or just anorexia. The term *anorexia nervosa* means loss of appetite. That definition, however, doesn't really fit. People with anorexia are hungry. They usually have a normal appetite. However, they deny their hunger. Instead of eating, they starve themselves. Sometimes people with anorexia exercise too much as well.

People with anorexia often drop below 85 percent of their ideal body weight. However, they don't see themselves as extremely thin. When they look in a mirror, they see someone who is fat. Anorexia can cause people to develop a distorted, or unreal, body image.

Myth: Every person who has an eating disorder is extremely underweight.

Fact: Many people with bulimia are of average weight or above. People with binge-eating disorder often are overweight.

Myth: Anorexia is a female's illness.

Fact: Males as well as females have anorexia.

Losing too much weight can lead to many other health problems for people with anorexia. They often lose their hair. They can have heart problems. Anorexia can cause people to grow fine hair on their arms, legs, and other body parts. This is their body's way of trying to keep itself warm when weight drops below a certain point.

Anorexia can cause depression and anxiety. It can lead to organ damage and bone mineral loss. Bone mineral loss can lead to osteoporosis, which causes bone mass to decrease. Osteoporosis can result in fragile bones that break easily. In the most serious cases, anorexia can cause death.

"I look at the girls in TV and magazine ads. Then I look at myself in the mirror. What I see is a fat girl!"
—Becca, age 15

"One day I just stopped eating. I didn't know what was going on. I just knew I didn't want to put food in my body."—Jake, age 16

Bulimia and Binge-Eating Disorder

Anorexia is only one type of eating disorder. Two other eating disorders are bulimia and binge-eating disorder.

People with bulimia binge, or eat a great amount of food at one time. Then they purge, or rid their body of food. They usually purge by vomiting, or throwing up, or using laxatives. A laxative is a drug that loosens the body's solid waste and allows it to be eliminated quickly. A person can have both anorexia and bulimia.

People with binge-eating disorder consume a great amount of food at one time. They cannot control the amount they eat. Unlike people with bulimia, people who have binge-eating disorder do not purge themselves. Compulsive overeating is another name for binge-eating disorder.

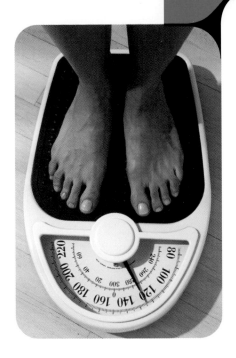

People with eating disorders often use food to block out uncomfortable feelings. They use food like alcoholics use liquor or drug addicts use heroin. Food can be like a drug to many people with eating disorders. An estimated 8 million Americans have eating disorders.

Teens Are at Risk

Teens especially are at risk for anorexia. A teen's body grows and changes rapidly during adolescence. Not all of these changes are welcome. Girls tend to gain weight during the teen years. Before puberty, or sexual maturity, boys and girls have about the same amount of body fat. At the end of puberty, girls often have twice as much body fat as before. The teen years are a time when many people try dieting for the first time. Dieting often is the first step for people who have anorexia.

Many teens are attracted to the idea of being extremely thin. However, they may not realize the dangers of starving themselves.

The Good News

Eating disorders are serious health conditions. They affect a person's physical and mental health. However, people with anorexia can learn the causes of their eating disorder. They can learn to change the way they think about food and their body. They can develop healthy eating habits. This book explains the facts about anorexia and how to cure it.

Filene woke up to the smell of muffins baking. She looked

FILENE, AGE 14

forward to breakfast. This was the third day in a row she could eat without feeling guilty. Her struggle with anorexia had taken months and the support of friends, family, and medical professionals. It had taken one small step after another. Her rules for eating had changed. She had been the one to change them. She was fighting a difficult battle, but she was determined to win it.

Points to Consider

What does the phrase *normal weight* mean to you? How did you decide what that weight is?

What do you think might cause a person who is not overweight to think he or she is fat?

What do you think is the difference between having a healthy appetite and compulsively overeating?

Anorexia affects more females than males. One out of every 200 young women in the United States has anorexia.

Teens are more at risk for anorexia than any other age group.

Certain activities and careers place a high value on being thin. Athletes, dancers, skaters, and performers especially are at risk for anorexia.

Anorexia may run in families.

Anorexia may have a physical or chemical basis.

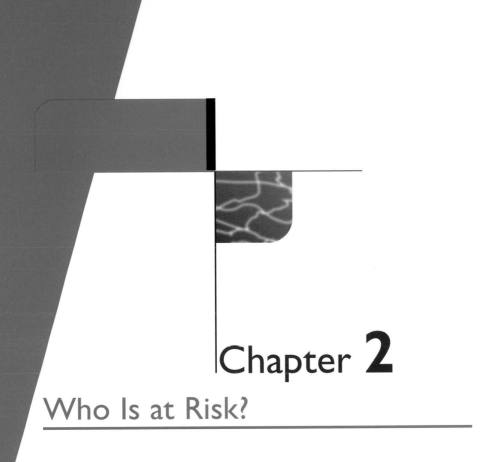

Chapter **2**

Who Is at Risk?

No single cause is responsible for anorexia. Many factors influence the development of this disorder. However, some people are more at risk for anorexia than others are. Researchers have identified several risk factors for anorexia, including gender, age, activity or career, and family. Physical or chemical factors also may play a role.

Gender

Females are more likely than males to have anorexia. In fact, about 90 percent of people with anorexia are female. Studies estimate that one out of every 200 young women has anorexia.

"I was tired of getting called names and being made fun of because I was fat. I decided to stop eating. It hurt less."—Walt, age 14

"I didn't recognize my sister when she came home from college. She looked like a skeleton. I'm afraid she has anorexia."—Yer Lee, age 13

"I'm a skater. Skaters can't be fat, so I count every calorie. I think about food all the time."—Mirabel, age 15

"I hate it when my dad yells at me. I hope I get so thin I'll just disappear."—Jen, age 17

However, males also can have anorexia. Currently, around 10 percent of people with anorexia are males. The number of males who have anorexia may be increasing. Males are more likely than females to hide their eating disorder. This means more males may have eating disorders than the numbers show.

Age

Teens are at greater risk for anorexia than any other age group. Eighty-five percent of anorexia occurs before age 20. In teens, anorexia is most likely to develop at age 12 or 13. The second most likely age when anorexia develops is around 17. Preteens also are at risk. In fact, more anorexia in children ages 8 to 11 is being reported each year.

One percent of teen girls in the United States has anorexia. Up to 10 percent of those girls may die as a result of it. Poor nutrition, lack of water, and organ damage can cause death.

Kendra's dance teacher gave her that look again. Kendra knew what it meant. She looked down at her stomach. Was it sticking out too much? The leotard showed everything. "I've got to lose 5 pounds before the recital," Kendra thought. Okay, she would skip breakfast and lunch again. She'd have just a salad for dinner. A dancer can't be fat.

Activity or Career

Anorexia occurs more often in people who are involved in certain activities or careers. More athletes, gymnasts, dancers, skaters, models, and actors have anorexia than people in other activities or careers. People involved in these activities or careers place a high value on looking thin and fit.

Experts estimate that 15 to 60 percent of athletes and performers have eating disorders. According to the American College of Sports Medicine, 62 percent of female athletes are at risk for an eating disorder.

Sometimes athletes compete not only on the field or in an event but also to lose weight. Many sports stress self-control over the body and mind. Molding the body through dieting and exercise may be seen as an accomplishment.

Young children are weight-conscious, too. Canadian children in grades 3 and 4 said they would rather lose a parent, get cancer, or live through nuclear war than be fat.

Family

Research has shown that anorexia may run in families. A parent, aunt, and cousin all may have the disorder. This suggests that some people may inherit the tendency to have anorexia. In one study, researchers found that 20 percent of people with anorexia had a family member with an eating disorder. In a study of twins, anorexia occurred in 9 of 16 identical twin children whose mother had anorexia. However, only 1 of 14 fraternal twin children of mothers with anorexia had the eating disorder.

Physical or Chemical Factors

Experts are working to find a link between a person's physical makeup and anorexia. Research suggests that the brain of a person with anorexia may not balance food intake with energy use. This means the person cannot tell when he or she needs food for energy. Other studies show that people with anorexia produce too much of a hormone that prevents weight gain. Hormones are chemicals that the body produces that control a person's growth and development.

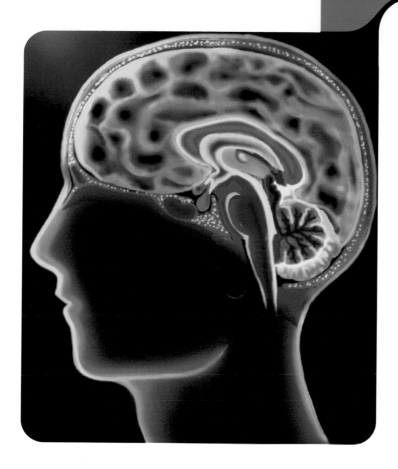

Points to Consider

Why do you think anorexia is more likely to develop in females than in males?

Teens are at high risk for anorexia. How do you think this could be prevented?

Name some of the pressures that dancers, skaters, gymnasts, and other athletes feel that may increase their risk for anorexia.

People with anorexia tend to share some personality and behavior traits. These include perfectionism, low self-esteem, problems expressing feelings, and fear of change.

People with anorexia also may have depression and obsessive-compulsive disorder.

Many people with anorexia have a distorted body image.

Family issues may play a part in the development of anorexia.

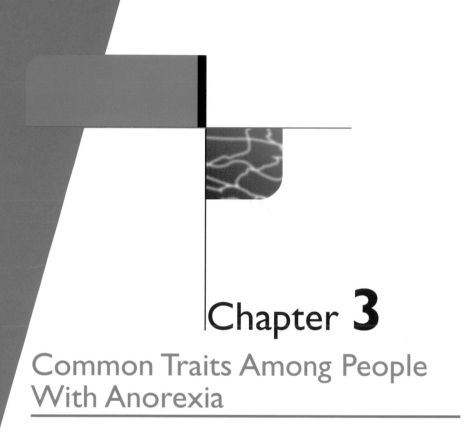

Chapter **3**

Common Traits Among People With Anorexia

All his life, Todd had been regarded as a good kid. Todd

TODD, AGE 14

never caused his parents any trouble. He always did well in school. He hardly ever got angry. Although most of the kids liked Todd, he didn't have any close friends.

When he was 14, Todd decided he needed to lose weight. He started dieting. He didn't stop. He started running every day to lose more weight. Several months later, Todd was admitted to the hospital. He weighed 65 pounds.

Some Common Traits Among People With Anorexia

People who study eating disorders have found that people with anorexia have some traits in common. These traits include perfectionism, low self-esteem, difficulty expressing emotions, and fear of change.

Perfectionism

Perfectionism is a trait of many people with anorexia. Perfectionism means trying to be the best in school and at sports or other activities. People who are perfectionists feel like they can't make a mistake. They feel guilty if they fail at something they try. They often think they have to please everyone.

No one is perfect. Everyone makes mistakes. Yet people who are perfectionists put pressure on themselves never to make mistakes. When they fail at something or disappoint others, they may feel out of control. Some may see starving themselves as a way to take back control. They alone decide what and how much they eat. They may see being thin as the only thing they can do right.

Low Self-Esteem

Many people with anorexia have low self-esteem. This means they don't value themselves or think they have much worth. People with low self-esteem often care too much about what others think. They think others' opinions are more important than their own.

For people with anorexia, low self-esteem can mean not liking or valuing their body. They may see being thin as a way to get others' approval.

Difficulty Expressing Emotions

People with anorexia often have difficulty recognizing and expressing their emotions. Everyone feels hurt or embarrassed once in a while. People with anorexia may feel ashamed to tell others when they have those feelings. They may fear others won't understand or approve.

The average teen needs about 1,800 to 2,500 calories each day to stay healthy. Some people with anorexia consume only 300 to 500 calories a day.

Many people with anorexia find it difficult to comfort themselves or others. They may feel they don't deserve to get sympathy or understanding from others when something goes wrong. It also may be hard for them to understand how others feel in such situations. They cannot put themselves in another's position.

Fear of Change

Many people are afraid of change. However, people with anorexia often find change terrifying. The fact is that the teen years are full of change. Often teens are not prepared for the changes in their body. They may not feel ready to accept adult responsibilities or make decisions about their future. Many of these changes are out of their control. Some teens with anorexia feel the only control they have is over what and how much they eat.

Other Factors

People with anorexia may have other illnesses as well. Depression and obsessive-compulsive disorder are illnesses that can co-occur with anorexia.

Depression

Depression is a serious illness in which feelings of sadness, hopelessness, and helplessness persist for more than two weeks. Feeling sad and afraid at times is part of life. For many people with anorexia, however, the feelings are overwhelming and last a long time. Depression is common in 40 to 80 percent of people with eating disorders. Major depression and mood disorders also can occur in the family of people with anorexia.

Obsessive-Compulsive Disorder

Some people with anorexia also have obsessive-compulsive disorder. This is a medical condition affecting the brain. It causes a person to become obsessed, or controlled, by certain thoughts or behaviors. People with anorexia may become obsessed with exercise, dieting, and food.

Obsessive thoughts can lead to a distorted body image. As people with anorexia become thinner, they still see themselves as fat. They deny health problems and behavior changes. People with anorexia may think about food constantly, but they cannot admit they are hungry.

"My relatives used to make rude comments about my being fat. I started dieting to show them."
—Steve, age 14

"We were having so many problems in our family. I felt so helpless. I couldn't do anything about them. I used to cry all the time. I started dieting. I still cried, but at least I was doing something."—Jenelle, age 16

RACHEL, AGE 17

Rachel wanted to lose a few pounds. Soon those few pounds became a dozen. A dozen pounds became 30 and then 50. One day when Rachel stepped on the scale, she weighed 80 pounds. She looked in the mirror and cried. How could she weigh only 80 pounds and still look fat?

Rachel started out with the idea of losing a few pounds. Then dieting itself became the goal. Even though the weight fell away, she was unable to see herself as anything but fat.

Family Issues

Some teens with anorexia have poor relationships with family members, particularly parents. They may feel that parents judge them too harshly or are too strict with them. They may feel pressure from parents to be or to act a certain way. Using food may be a way to deal with their feelings of resentment and anger toward a parent.

In some families, communicating thoughts or feelings does not happen easily. Family members may have difficulty talking with each other about their problems. A teen's eating disorder may not be recognized or noticed. Sometimes the teen's eating disorder becomes a way of expressing his or her unhappiness.

"Why didn't you make the team?" Carl's dad asked him.

CARL, AGE 16

"Aren't you as good as the rest? You're always practicing." Carl shrugged. "Well, talk to the coach. See if he'll give you another chance. And quit pushing your food around on your plate. Eat, for heaven's sake!"

AT A GLANCE

Symptoms of anorexia:

Losing a lot of weight in a relatively short time

Continuing to diet even though extremely thin

Feeling dissatisfied with appearance and believing the body is fat, even when extremely underweight

Cessation, or stopping, of menstrual periods in females

Having unusual eating habits

Being fascinated with food

Eating in secret

Exercising obsessively

Feeling depressed

Points to Consider

What is the difference between wanting to do your best and being a perfectionist? How could being a perfectionist cause problems for someone?

Why do you think some people have trouble expressing how they feel? What are some of the ways you express sadness or anger?

Change is a part of life. Can you think of something that has changed in your life recently? How did you feel about it? What did you do?

Do you think there is an ideal way to look? Where do you think this ideal came from?

Chapter

Overview

Our culture places a high value on being thin. Many people with anorexia think that being thin will make them happy and successful.

Both the mind and body play a part in anorexia.

Many people with anorexia feel out of control. They may use food, dieting, and weight control to feel powerful.

Research shows that people with anorexia lack the proper amount of some chemicals and nutrients in their body. These imbalances could contribute to a person becoming anorexic or could result from anorexia.

Stress also may be a cause of anorexia.

Chapter 4

What Causes Anorexia?

Dawn leafed through her favorite magazine. All the models were stick thin. She glanced at the TV. The female stars looked thin and glamorous. Dawn looked down at her thighs. She pinched the skin around her waist. "Wow, I'd better knock off the ice cream and chips," she thought.

DAWN, AGE 15

In the Fiji Islands off the coast of Australia, big women were considered beautiful. After television arrived in 1995, Fiji girls began talking about diets. By 1998, Fiji girls said they felt "too big" or "fat."

A Thin Figure Is Not the Key to Happiness

In North American culture, being thin is in. Being overweight is out. However, the messages are mixed. Magazines, TV, and billboards show beautiful, thin people having fun. Those same media are filled with advertisements for fast food, snack food, and drinks. On the one hand, people are told that being thin is desirable. On the other hand, they are being told to eat, eat, eat.

Most people choose to eat what they want over being thin. For many, the desire for food is stronger than the desire to be thin. People with anorexia, however, may see being thin as the key to success and happiness. Food is the enemy that prevents them from achieving their goal. They starve themselves to be thin. What may start as a diet to lose a few pounds turns into an obsession. People with problems such as depression or low self-esteem may think their life will improve if only they are thin. They might believe that losing weight is a magical solution to their problems.

Sadly, most people with anorexia focus all their attention on their body. They can't think about anything but food, dieting, and weight. These obsessive thoughts only cover up other problems explained in Chapter 3.

Both Mind and Body

Anorexia is an illness that involves both the mind and body. People with anorexia often use dieting and weight management to feel in control mentally and emotionally. However, anorexia also may have a physical basis. Chemical imbalances have been found in people with anorexia. Stress also may play a role in the development of anorexia.

"Carmen, have you lost weight? You're as thin as a model!"

CARMEN, AGE 14

Carmen smiled. Finally, someone noticed. Her diet was working. She pulled her apple out of her lunch sack. Then she sliced it in tiny pieces. Every day she had just an apple for lunch. She always sliced it into as many pieces as she could. She would eat each tiny piece one at a time.

A study of more than 3,000 young people in grades 5 through 8 showed that more than 40 percent felt fat or wanted to lose weight. Only 20 percent actually were overweight.

A Matter of Control

People with anorexia often feel helpless and out of control. For them, taking control of what and how much they eat gives them a sense of power. They may not feel this way in any other part of their life.

Engaging in food rituals is one way people with anorexia take control. Carmen's lunch became a type of food ritual. She always ate the same thing in the same way. Food rituals can be a danger sign of anorexia.

Food often is fascinating to people with anorexia. They may offer to cook for others even while they refuse to eat. However, they often are secretive about their own food habits and may choose to eat alone.

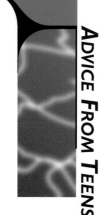
"Here's my advice. Like yourself. Then you won't change for others—even to be thin. Besides, people who like you just because you're thin aren't worth it."
—Mia, age 14

"Who's telling me I'm supposed to be thin, anyway? I think it's a crock. Somebody's just trying to sell me something. Personally, I'm not going to buy it."
—Erin, age 18

Chemical and Nutritional Imbalances

The body needs certain chemicals and nutrients to function normally. Nutrients are substances such as vitamins, minerals, and protein that people need to stay healthy. Research shows that some of these chemicals and nutrients are missing or out of balance in people with anorexia. Experts aren't sure if the imbalances cause the eating disorder or if the disorder causes the imbalances.

Zinc

Studies have shown a possible link between zinc and anorexia. Zinc is an important mineral found in red and white meat and shellfish. Too little zinc in the body can result in reduced growth and sexual development. It also can cause skin problems and weaken the immune system. This means a person has a low resistance to illness. Researchers have found that many people with anorexia are zinc-deficient. This means they have too little zinc in their body.

Experts are not sure whether the zinc deficiency is caused by anorexia or is a result of the disorder. More studies are being done to find the answer.

Serotonin

Research suggests that low serotonin levels may play a role in causing anorexia. Serotonin is a neurotransmitter, or substance that sends signals from the nerves to the brain. Serotonin controls a person's mood and appetite. Some people with anorexia have serotonin levels that do not function normally. As a result, losing weight may improve their mood and make them feel calm. The weight loss reduces their serotonin levels and improves their mood and behavior.

Stress

Studies show that stress can cause chemical imbalances in people. Stress also may be a factor in causing anorexia and other eating disorders. Stressful events have affected most people's eating habits at one time or another. Some people might lose their appetite after hearing bad news or breaking up with their boyfriend or girlfriend. Others might react to such an event by stuffing themselves with food to avoid painful feelings. However, a person at risk for anorexia may stop eating for a day or two and like the feeling. The person may decide to continue not eating. That may be the first step in the illness.

Are your eating habits normal? If you answer yes to any of these questions, your eating habits may be dangerous to your health.

Do you restrict your diet to a low number of calories a day?

Do you spend a lot of time thinking about food? Do you read about it, prepare it, and count calories?

Do you feel disgusted about your weight even though others say you are thin?

Are you uncomfortable or embarrassed about your food habits?

Do you deceive others about your eating habits?

Do you have unusual eating rituals?

Do you fear you won't be able to stop eating once you start?

Points to Consider

Why do you think our culture values thinness so much? Where do you think this value comes from?

People with anorexia often believe if they are thin enough, people will like them. Do you think this works? Why or why not?

What are some of the things you can't control in your life? What are some things that you can control?

Anorexia can damage a person's self-esteem and relationships. Family and friends may not know how to help.

The body suffers when it isn't fed properly. Some organs may shut down. This can cause permanent damage and even death.

The person with anorexia may feel guilt and shame.

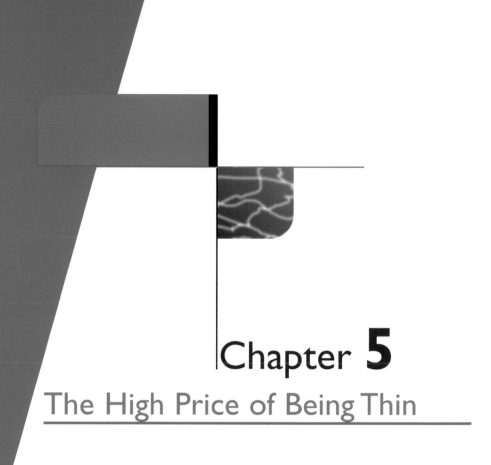

Chapter **5**

The High Price of Being Thin

People with anorexia pay a high price for being thin. Often they don't realize that their need for control can cost them their health and even their life.

"When I was starving myself, it made me feel special. I was doing something no one else could do. People looked at me with awe. They couldn't see what was going on inside me."—Maria, age 17

"Look at you," LaRay said. "How do you do it? How do you

DARLA, AGE 18

stay so thin? You're incredible. While the rest of us pig out, you stick to your fruit and veggies. You're amazing, Darla. I've never seen anyone with as much willpower!"

"LaRay says I have willpower," Darla thinks. "If only she knew I'm shaking inside. I wonder what she'd think if she saw my hair coming off my head in clumps in the shower. I wonder what she'd say about the weird little hairs I have growing all over my body. I'm scared I'm doing something terrible to myself. But I just can't eat. I can't."

The Price

Anorexia is a serious illness. Starvation takes a great toll on a person's body and mind. Relationships suffer as well. Family and friends often don't know what to do. They feel frustrated and angry about the person's slow dance with self-destruction. The family may try to force the person to eat. This almost never works. The person with anorexia feels even more alone and misunderstood.

Grant is a wrestler. He has to keep his weight down. He has always liked the challenge of keeping the pounds off. He weighs himself several times a day to make sure he's never over his limit. But lately he has noticed that he is always cold. His hands and feet never seem to warm up. His skin itches, too. It is so dry that it has begun to flake.

Physical Effects of Anorexia

The body needs food in the right amounts to work properly. When the body is deprived of food, it will slow itself down to conserve its small energy supply. When people with anorexia reach a dangerously low weight, their body begins to shut down. They may experience the conditions listed on the following page.

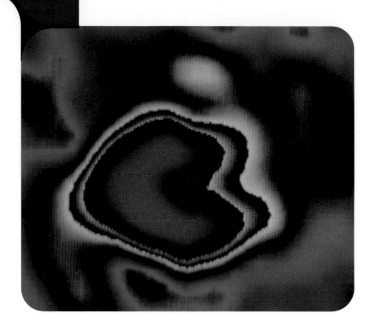

- Soft, fine hair growth over much of the body

- Menstruation, or periods, stopping in females

- Dry, flaky skin

- Loss of scalp hair

- Sensitivity to cold

- Abnormal weight loss

- Bloating and constipation, or difficulty eliminating solid waste from the body

Anorexia causes changes inside the body as well. All body organs, including the brain, can be affected. When the body has lost 40 percent of its weight required to maintain health, organs lose weight as well. They give up their substance to provide fuel to keep the body running.

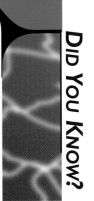
Some of these internal changes to body organs are listed below. Many arc life-threatening. In fact, 10 percent of people with severe, untreated anorexia die.

The pancreas, an organ that produces insulin to handle the sugar a person eats, may malfunction or shut down. This often causes symptoms, or signs, of diabetes.

The kidneys may be permanently damaged. This is caused by vitamin deficiencies, dehydration, or infection. Dehydration occurs when a person does not consume enough liquids. A person whose kidneys are damaged seriously may require a kidney transplant.

Anemia may develop, causing extreme weakness and fatigue. Anemia results when the body doesn't have enough oxygen-carrying blood cells.

Too little fat in the body can deprive the heart of the vitamins and minerals it needs to function. This can weaken the heart and result in a heart attack.

Pop singer Karen Carpenter had anorexia for eight years. She died of heart failure at age 32. The most common cause of death in a person with long-term anorexia is low serum potassium. This means there is a low level of potassium in the blood. Low serum potassium can cause an irregular heartbeat.

Severe anorexia can result in irregular pumping rhythms in the heart. This can lead to dangerously low blood pressure.

Damage to nerves can result in sudden attacks called seizures. Nerve damage also can cause tingling or loss of feeling in hands and feet.

Mental and Emotional Effects of Anorexia

Starvation affects a person's ability to think clearly. When a person's brain becomes malnourished, thinking can become confused and distorted. A person with anorexia may become unusually fascinated by food. The person may carefully inspect a cracker before breaking it into bits. Then he or she may eat only a crumb. Food both attracts and repels.

As the illness progresses, people with anorexia no longer see themselves as a whole person. They see only their hips, their legs, or their waist. They may become so obsessed with their mission to lose weight that they withdraw from others. They may become severely depressed. People with anorexia feel shame and guilt for their behavior. They often think that no one understands them. What they need most is help and understanding.

Points to Consider

Why do you think people who lose weight think they are accomplishing something?

When does dieting become dangerous?

Why might a person with anorexia be reluctant to eat around other people?

Why do you think some people with anorexia keep on dieting even though their body shows signs of starvation?

Treatment for anorexia involves three steps. These include treating medical problems, restoring normal weight, and treating emotional causes.

Weight gain is achieved by eating healthy foods in the right amounts and exercising moderately.

The underlying emotional causes of anorexia can be explored through individual, family, and group therapy.

The mineral zinc is sometimes used as a nutritional supplement in treating anorexia. However, antidepressants have not been used successfully.

Chapter **6**

Steps in Treatment

"The hardest part is telling someone you have a problem. I finally decided to tell my pastor. After church one day, I just hung around the youth room. He asked if something was wrong. That's when I just blurted it out.

LUCAS, AGE 15

"It was embarrassing, but I couldn't stop crying. He was so understanding. He helped me get an appointment with a doctor. Then I began to see a therapist. She's easy to talk to. But I'm so glad I told my pastor. That's when things started to get better. I'm still not there, but I'm working at it."

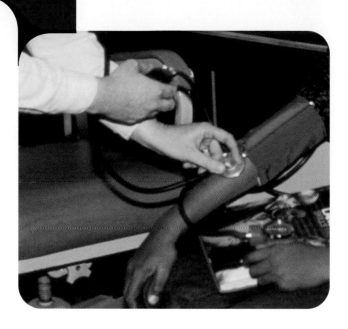

The first step in treating anorexia often is the most difficult one. The person with anorexia must admit that he or she needs help. Many people with anorexia deny they have a problem. Others may not notice the problem until the person is extremely thin or has obvious health problems. The disorder may not be diagnosed until it is in an advanced stage. This makes treatment more difficult.

Treatment for anorexia involves three steps. Each step requires the professional help of physicians, nutrition specialists, and counselors. First, the person must be evaluated for any urgent medical problems. If problems are found, they must be treated immediately. The next step is to help the person begin gaining weight by establishing healthy eating and exercise habits. Third, the person must be treated for the psychological causes of the anorexia.

Experts advise 10 to 12 weeks for full nutritional recovery from anorexia. Dietary supplements such as vitamins and minerals usually are not recommended. The goal is to obtain necessary nutrients through healthy eating.

Treating Medical Problems

A doctor will determine through a physical exam if the person with anorexia needs urgent medical treatment. Some of these medical problems were listed in Chapter 5. Any life-threatening conditions must be treated immediately. Sometimes a hospital stay is necessary. This is usually the case if a person has:

- Body weight that is 20 percent below what is required to maintain health

- Disturbed or irregular heart rhythms

- Severe depression

- Extremely low blood pressure

Achieving and Maintaining Normal Weight

Recovery for a person with anorexia involves gaining weight, learning healthy eating habits, and exercising moderately.

Gaining Weight

A person with anorexia must be put on a program to gain weight. A physician usually sets the weight goal, which is generally one or two pounds a week. Gaining weight can be difficult. To the person with anorexia, gaining weight can feel like giving up.

The person with anorexia is eased back into normal eating habits gradually. He or she may be required to eat a certain number of meals each day. The requirements may change daily to work more calories into the diet. In severe anorexia, the physician may choose to hospitalize the person to make sure the weight goal is met. Intravenous feeding may be necessary to achieve the weight goal. When this happens, doctors use a tube to inject nutrients and calories into the person's blood veins.

Learning Healthy Eating Habits

The person recovering from anorexia must learn new, healthy eating habits. Dietitians help both the person and his or her family to learn about nutrition. These experts are trained in diet and nutrition. They help set nutritional goals and suggest ways to plan meals. They help the person to understand the importance of eating healthful foods in the right amounts.

"The second time I went to the hospital, I admitted myself. I was sick of being sick. I wanted to get better. Everyone was nice, but it still wasn't easy being there. Many times I didn't want to do what I was told. But I did, because I knew what would happen if I didn't. I knew I might die, and I didn't want to."
—Kimberly, age 14

Exercising Moderately

Many people with anorexia are compulsive exercisers. This means they exercise too much. Their exercise habits may have contributed to their illness. The doctor may limit the person's exercise during the first stages of treatment for anorexia. However, some exercise may help reduce stomach and intestinal distress. These problems often occur with changes in a person's diet.

"I knew I had a problem. I just didn't know why. And I didn't know what to do about it. In our family, we never talked about feelings. If I got mad at my mom or dad, I just stuffed it. I didn't think I could tell them. Through counseling, I've learned this was part of my problem. Now I'm learning to say how I feel. My family is in counseling, too. It has helped a lot."

MICKIE, AGE 16

Talking It Out Through Therapy

Treating the mental and emotional problems that contribute to anorexia is essential to a person's recovery. This is the job of mental health professionals. These professionals help the person with anorexia understand and cope with his or her illness. Help is available through individual, family, and group therapy.

In individual therapy, the person learns to understand the emotions that trigger eating disorders. Psychologists, or specialists who study the mind and emotions, help the person overcome fear of gaining weight. Together they discuss ways to deal with fears of food and eating. Treatment also focuses on improving body image and self-esteem.

Family therapy also is important in treatment for anorexia. Family members meet with a counselor to learn ways to offer support to the person with anorexia. The family also can gain a better understanding of the disease and its causes.

Group therapy often works well for teens. Most teens will discuss their problems more freely with other teens than they will with adults. The person with anorexia can meet others who have the same problem. Group members help each other deal with their illness.

The Case Against Antidepressants

While zinc has been shown to be helpful for anorexia, drugs such as antidepressants have not been successful. Antidepressants are used to treat depression, which often is a symptom of anorexia. However, many antidepressants suppress the appetite. This works against the person with anorexia who is trying to gain weight. In many cases, weight gain and the body's recovery of normal functions help improve the person's depression.

Taking It Slow

Successful treatment of anorexia depends on a program that fits the person's needs. A person recovering from anorexia may continue to think about weight and food. He or she may slip back into poor eating patterns. Full recovery takes time.

Points to Consider

Why do you think it might be difficult for someone to admit he or she has an eating disorder?

Imagine you know someone with anorexia who is seriously malnourished. Is it more important to deal first with medical problems or emotional issues? Why?

Why do you think it is important for the family of a person with anorexia to participate in treatment?

Helping a person with anorexia may be difficult because he or she may be unwilling to admit to the problem.

You can do many things to help a person who you suspect has anorexia. You can offer support, talk with an adult you trust, and educate yourself.

You can help yourself if you think you have anorexia. You can change the way you talk to yourself, confide in someone you trust, and ask for help. You also can learn more about eating disorders.

Chapter **7**

What You Can Do

Many people with anorexia do not admit they have a problem. This makes it difficult for others to help. However, most people with anorexia need help to stop starving themselves. Without help, they risk their health and their life.

"Don't be afraid to ask for help. I did, and it saved my life."—Marlys, age 15

"Don't be so concerned about what other people think."—LaToya, age 17

"Become more social. Get involved."—David, age 16

"Look at Allain!" whispered Nola. "What is up with her? Her gym shorts are practically falling off!"

ALLAIN, AGE 17

"I know," replied Lisa. "I'll bet she's lost 20 pounds since the beginning of the year. It's kind of scary. We both sit at the same lunch table, only she never eats a thing. The other day I asked her if she was okay. I told her she looked so thin. She just said she was fine, she'd been running a lot for track. I don't believe it, though. I think she might have anorexia. I wish I knew what to do."

If Someone You Know Needs Help

Many teens know someone who has an eating disorder. Do you suspect a friend or family member has anorexia? You want to help, but what can you do? Look again at the warning signs of anorexia listed in Chapter 3.

First, it's important to realize that you cannot cure the person's illness. Anorexia is a symptom of other problems. In many cases, the person is using anorexia as a way to cope with those problems. It is important for the person to deal with the causes of anorexia first. Only then can he or she learn to change unhealthy eating behaviors.

You can help a friend or family member who has anorexia. You can show you care and talk with the person about your concern. It's helpful to be a good listener. You can talk about your own problems, too. This lets the person know he or she is not the only one with worries.

Here are a few other things you might do:

Avoid talking about weight and food. Don't point out how little the person eats. He or she needs your friendship, not criticism.

Avoid remarks about appearance. Instead, give compliments that have nothing to do with appearance. For example, say, "I didn't know you could play the saxophone that well! We were all talking about it at lunch."

Don't get discouraged. People with anorexia often don't trust others. You may feel rejected from time to time. However, don't give up. Studies show that people who recover from anorexia credit their recovery most to a caring person in their life.

Anorexia nervosa was first defined as a medical problem in 1873. However, descriptions of people starving themselves have been around since medieval times.

Tell the person how much you care. Explain that you are not judging the person because he or she has an eating disorder.

Talk about your concern with a trusted adult, such as the school nurse or a guidance counselor. He or she might not be aware of the person's anorexia and may be able to help.

Educate yourself. The more you learn about anorexia, the more you can help. The For More Information and Useful Addresses and Internet Sites sections at the back of this book can help you.

If You Need Help

Perhaps you believe you have anorexia. You have taken the first step toward getting help. Admitting to yourself that you may have a problem is a big step. People with anorexia often want to be helped but don't know how to ask for it.

You've learned in this book that anorexia has many causes. Some have a psychological basis. The causes can relate to the way you think about yourself.

You might try changing how you talk to yourself. Here are some things you can say to yourself:

It's okay to worry.

It's okay to talk about my problems.

It's okay to have a good time.

I don't want food running my life.

I don't have to get on the scale every day.

I can figure out why I'm angry or sad.

I don't have to worry about what people think of me.

I can accept compliments.

I have many good qualities.

I don't have to be thin. Who says thin is beautiful, anyway? And who says they're right?

You can do more than change your self-talk. Here are a few other suggestions:

Contact the resources in the Useful Addresses and Internet Sites section at the back of this book. These organizations can help you.

Read the books suggested in the For More Information section at the back of this book.

Talk with someone you trust.

Don't be afraid to ask for help. Asking for help is a sign of strength, not weakness.

Know that there are many people who can and want to help you.

Take one small step now. You and many other people will be glad you did.

Points to Consider

How would you help a friend who told you that he or she had anorexia?

Think of two adults you could talk with about anorexia. What would you say to them if you suspect a friend has anorexia?

Why is recognizing and admitting to a problem the first step in solving it?

Glossary

binge (BINJ)—to eat a large amount of food in a short period of time

binge-eating disorder (BINJ EET-ing diss-OR-dur)—an eating disorder in which the person eats a large amount of food in a short time; also known as compulsive overeating.

bulimia (buh-LEEM-ee-uh)—an eating disorder in which the person overeats and then rids the body of food

dietitian (dye-uh-TI-shuhn)—a person who helps determine the proper kinds and amounts of food for a healthful diet

malnourishment (mal-NUR-ish-ment)—the body's condition when the right kinds or amounts of food are not consumed

nutrient (NOO-tree-uhnt)—a substance necessary for plants and animals, including humans, to stay strong and healthy

obsession (uhb-SESH-uhn)—an idea, thought, or emotion that is always on a person's mind

physician (fuh-ZISH-uhn)—a person with a medical degree who treats injured and sick people

psychological (sye-kuh-LOJ-uh-kuhl)—having to do with the mind or emotions

purge (PURJ)—to rid the body of food through vomiting or use of laxatives

self-esteem (self-uh-STEEM)—valuing and respecting oneself; feeling self-worth.

therapy (THER-uh-pee)—any procedure designed to improve a person's health or well-being

For More Information

Bode, Janet. *Food Fight: A Guide to Eating Disorders for Pre-Teens and Their Parents.* New York: Simon & Schuster, 1997.

Graves, Bonnie. *Bulimia.* Mankato, MN: Capstone Press, 2000.

Hornbacher, Marya. *Wasted: A Memoir of Anorexia and Bulimia.* New York: HarperCollins, 1998.

Nadelson, Carol C. *Anorexia Nervosa: Starving for Attention.* Broomall, PA: Chelsea House, 1998.

Peacock, Judith. *Compulsive Overeating.* Mankato, MN: Capstone Press, 2000.

Useful Addresses and Internet Sites

American Anorexia Bulimia Association
165 West 46th Street, Suite 1108
New York, NY 10036
www.aabainc.org

Anorexia Nervosa and Related Eating
Disorders (ANRED)
PO Box 5102
Eugene, OR 97405
www.anred.com

Eating Disorders Awareness and Prevention
(EDAP)
603 Stewart Street, Suite 803
Seattle, WA 98101
1-800-931-2237
www.edap.org

National Association of Anorexia Nervosa and
Associated Disorders (ANAD)
PO Box 7
Highland Park, IL 60035
www.anad.org

The National Eating Disorder Information
Centre
200 Elizabeth Street, CW1-211
Toronto, ON M5G 2C4
CANADA
www.nedic.on.ca

Eating Disorders Shared Awareness (EDSA)
New York
www.something-fishy.com
Provides information about eating disorders
and treatment, and provides tips for helping
friends and family members

Eating Disorders Shared Awareness (EDSA)
Canada
www.mirror-mirror.org/eatdis.htm
Canadian site for information on eating
disorders, treatment centers in Canada, U.S.,
and Ireland; includes survivors' stories.

Index

Index continued